AF326605

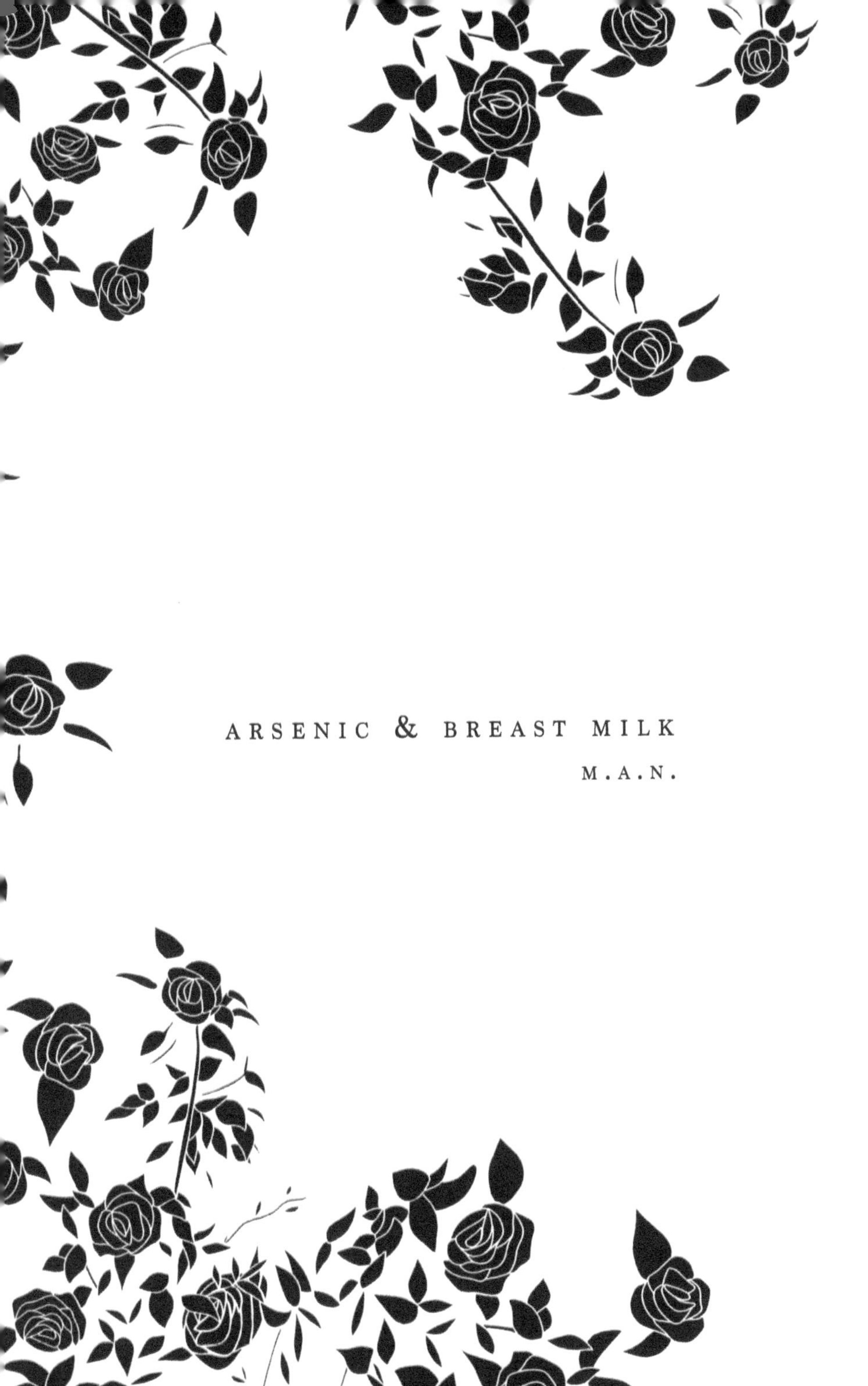

ARSENIC & BREAST MILK

M.A.N.

OTHER TITLES
& PUBLICATIONS

charlotte and the wooden castle
a novella

other magazine
founder/editor-in-chief
art & literature anthology

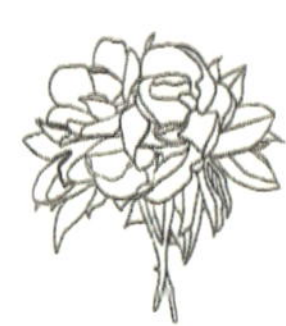

Published by Belletwine Press in 2018

Editing, Illustration & Design
by Michelle Athena Norton

Printing & Distribution
by IngramSpark

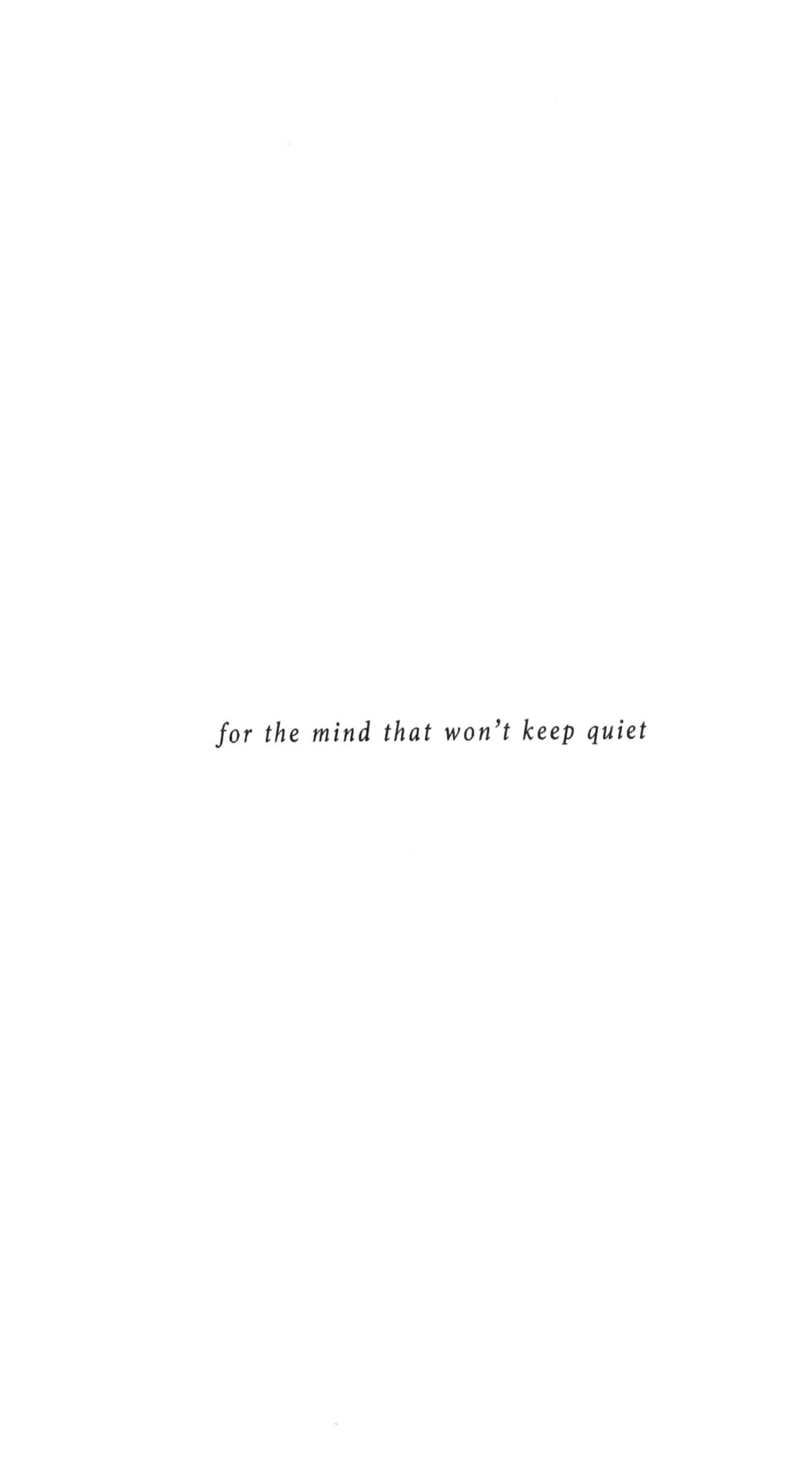

for the mind that won't keep quiet

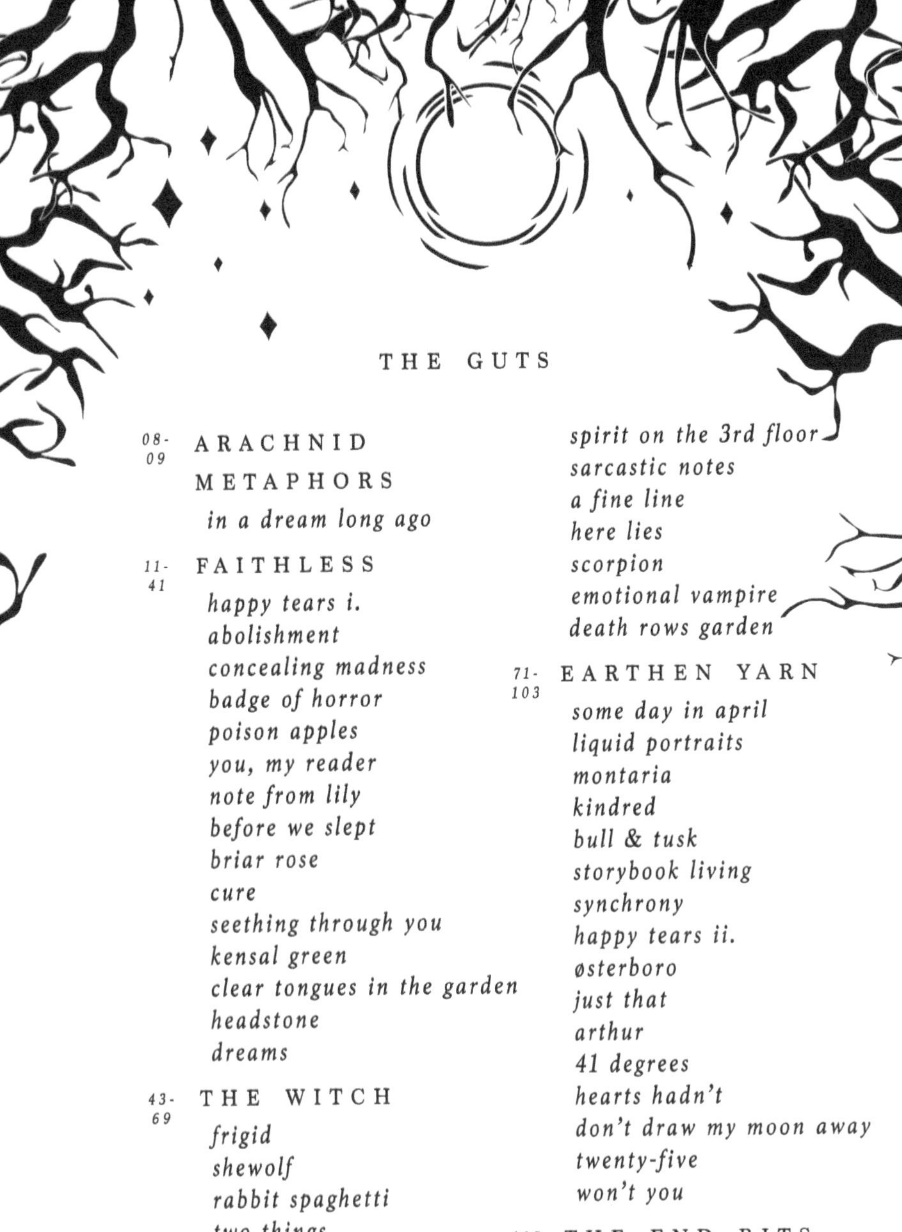

THE GUTS

ARACHNID METAPHORS

In a dream long ago,

I became lodged inside my own throat. It started
young, this recurring removal and relocation of my
mind. The feeling consumed me, as I had, in a way,
consumed myself. The placement of my consciousness
left me trapped where light was scarce, where wisps
of silken webs scaled the flesh inside my gullet. It
was as if my corporeal self had begun to rot and
a cosmic mistake had been made, one that left me
behind to bear witness to my own disintegration.

What a foul end, I would lament.

Countless attempts at escape provoked a stampede of
spiders to rush upward from my belly. They would
trample my minds eye; switching off the dull light,
illuminating abandonment in my spit-riddled cavern.
Then the little devils would overtake the walls, my
tongue like a wild beast invoking a tide of flesh
onto the invaders. The movement of their small feet
tickled like a swig of carbonation, and I would strike
until their limbs were broken and mashed, stuck
between my teeth like poppy seeds.

Abruptly I would wake, my hand quick to grip my
neck; the subconscious crossed from imaginary
recesses back into movement. My mouth continued
to salivate while my tongue explored curiously along
my molars.

Into the morning hours, I would speculate its
meaning; this periodic entrapment. Like clockwork,
the dream would come again, especially at any
conjured memory of it—I can still feel that frantic
discomfort—I never could quite grasp the signature
of its peculiarity. It was already washed away, soaked
into my core again. Like tracking a fawn in the
rain, I would exist temporarily in its nightmarish
gloom...until the rush and the chomping of arachnid
metaphors brought me back.

By some design, I revisit it now: a cobwebbed throat
and misplaced mind. Resumed for poetry. It is the
kind of courage that provokes a flight of demons
to achieve a realignment of feeling. This book is
the awakening; the moment where fear is disposed
for becoming oneself again and forever. No longer
circling doubt, I have found what I was looking for,
and hope, somewhere in these pages, you will too.

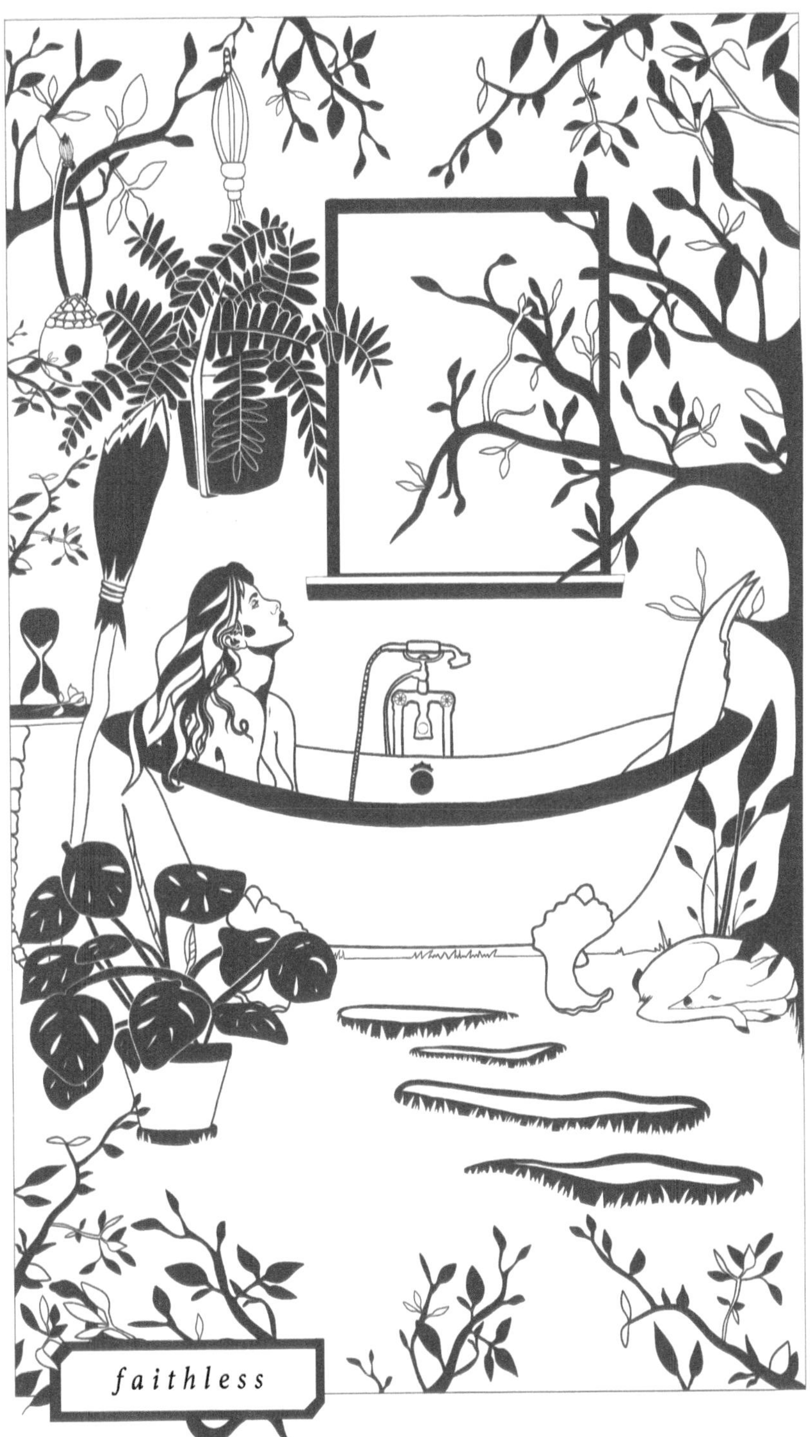
faithless

HAPPY TEARS I.

I'm weaning off bitterness,
splashing Joy into tombs
with a grip like jungle vines.
intermingling the soul's fabric
with earthen yarn, threaded loosely—
room left for sadness and pain,
shadows that let it happen,
single, unanticipated motions,
knees on gravel, an unstoppable rotation,
my heart's axis turning toward light—
I don't want to dry out.

ABOLISHMENT

bask in my shade,
said the sacred tree,
inhale my blossoms
and arrange my leaves,
turn out your hand
and carry my seeds
on to somewhere calm
with rainfall and breeze.
then Child, I will root
beneath to a salty sea,
among sunshine & sisters,
let your worries sleep.

CONCEALING MADNESS

she's quick to fall
torn from slumber
by imaginary princes
with a love like
unearthed magma
spilling lava over
wooden lambs

she cuts herself down
from woven nooses
collected like
dreamcatchers
on lost oaks
these aching arms
grasping weakly at
silent politicians

she's sane and wild
resurrected again after
hearing *all of you*
with scars like
phantom limbs
demanding answers from
windup boys

BADGE OF HORROR

girls like me are rooted
in solemn plots and refusal
to be anything but a grim reaper,
a dragon guarding virgin troves,
the collector of souls who fear her
and secrets no one knows.

POISON APPLES

miss defined-by-dysfunction,
what did you plan to be?
        climbing history's limbs
        with hand-me-down cleats?
        skidding, shaving bark
        from your diseased family tree,
the whole world smiles at you,
but they don't really see
        there's a parasite inside,
        my savior, these circles go wide,
can you magick my splinters to walking sticks,
a wand, somewhere to hide?
        for what supports, divides,
        concerned eyes peering out,
from greener pastures
beyond to a cliff;
        to you, miss trouble devout.
        you're a had-no-choice kid, they said,
        a *lesson in cuffs,*
jump or sail away
devil,
        you scream when it's enough.
        remain rooted or rot
reduced to a stump,
let's please,
        please start again,
        be gentle and repot.
but you run,
far enough that you stop and you
        pray, life's not what I thought,
        I'll die but not today,
tell stories to yourself
of victory and defeat,
        ask the stars and heavens,
        "why can't I breathe?"
remember the climb,
the pine needles and leaves,
        cling to the sap,
        your sweetness to be freed.

YOU, MY READER

you, my dear,
are a rarity; there is no
spring or summer deity
restricting your bloom.
you, eternal lumen, with
your healing heart strings
changing tune
to finer wisdoms
and waxing moons.

NOTE FROM LILY

fearsome thing with
unstoppable rage, she's powerful.
for, she does not crawl,
she claws from the holes
they buried her in.

she's a trauma-time-capsule
for a future generation to dig up;
these bodies *like her*
who will bear them,
trafficking billions, theft for a story;
crooks trading prestigious colors
blended by tearful eyes,
those that saw truth in the delusion,
salvation in the hallucination.

she is only great once she has gone;
an untouchable while she breathes,
pumped with arsenic and breast milk,
she's a life-giving self-sacrifice.

how was jesus not a woman?

BEFORE WE SLEPT

    ricocheting echoes,
that whimsy-induced pleasure
for a taste
    it lingers until morning,
that impossible feeling I sought
for the fear
    it lied with the lying
that constant perfecting of reasons
for why god
    this should have been easy
all along

BRIAR ROSE

locked in the tower of my own mind,
there's dust and shells with no sea for miles,
and the treetops, they feel like wanton daggers
preparing me for infrequent visits, unjust
daydreams broken things stirring staring seething
at a world without me, an imagination realm of
girls hoping, wishing for princes,
burning straw bounties, exclaiming fondly
long live the queen! heads will roll,
if they ever let me out, or perhaps die,
I'll grow wings join the owls and wake myself

CURE

a room full of
predatory glances
and glasses filled
with shades of desperation
these creatures citing blooms
of unlaid tombs
the memory is dug up
of the girl I used to be
I look down to my nails
dark with the grit of the fight
sharpened to take evidence of you
and I drown it out again

SEETHING THROUGH YOU

you asked for *just a little bit of patience,*
wasn't I the one telling you *I hate this?*
oh, you're right, *neither one of us was blameless*
but it feels like you're the one the shame fits.
spreading lies we both want the other painless
while I'm begging you through tears, *explain this,*
say the reason seething through you,
admit that you're faithless,
let's set the record straight now: you enter, the devil spits;
you lured me to love you, gave me a knife to slit my wrists,
every lie you spewed became a poison to get high with;
because I should leave and *I don't love you now, if I ever did.*

KENSAL GREEN

to soak; we absorb while we shed
hours of bliss-filled filth

but there's chaos,
chatter and whimpers around me
as i think back to the drip of the faucet;
the coo of metal handles turning,
the chirp of my muscles
to lavender salve

these are not birds
intruding on my nudity
from the stone sill,
for their voices are noise
drowning out song
while I ache in perpetual
social nakedness

these are not trees
casting curious shadows
onto the milky water,
for our forms do not sway
so inherently god-filled
while I filter keenly which
of us are monsters

we combat our ugliness,
fashioning beauty and
potions and pills
disrupting tranquility
for grandeur until we're
alone and

undress into a basin of
our long lost paradise

CLEAR TONGUES IN THE GARDEN

honest like I promised,
freed by a folded letter
in a mural of forgotten things,
the truth gaping wide,
my bare feet nestle here.

HEADSTONE

raven or crow by reputation;
both sinister and looming,
calls mocked sins mimicked,
but why not loyal, unreserved,
fearless in graveyard strolls
and a bearable witness to death?
for she catches and plucks *(if need be)*
the eyes of the musing & awakened

DREAMS

with eyes bent up and over the sightline of All;
of you, in your fragile way, strong and bendable,

your hold here is fleeting because
you are up there with the infinite,

your feet lift from the ground and
I spin you in blue light

gone and I remember
I never knew you.

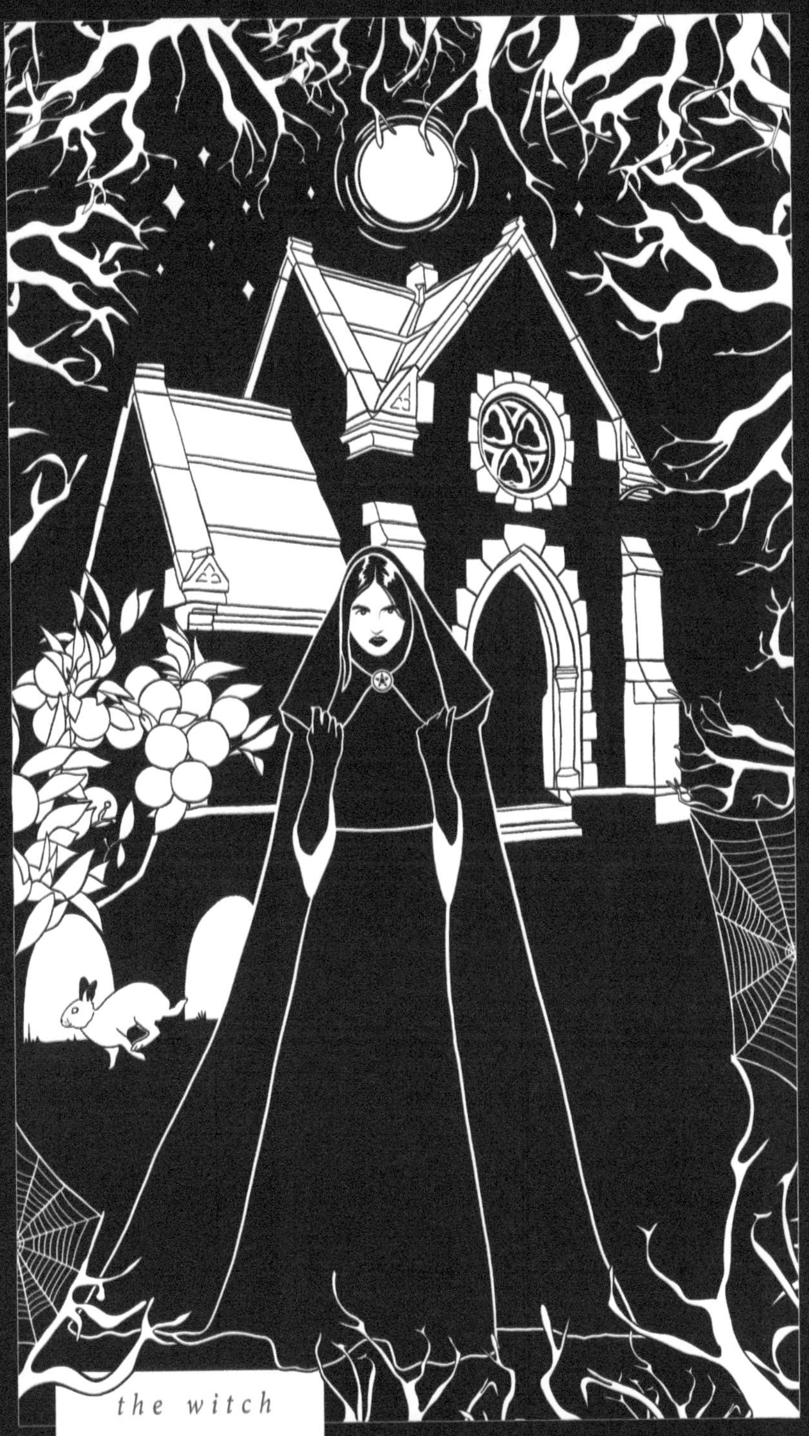
the witch

FRIGID

she kept the bathwater searing;
she liked to feel everything and nothing.
just like that, she floated in perpetual unease,
until it all cooled and she resented it.
just like you, she'd rise and drip, never clean,
until it all evaporated and she hated herself.

she kept the house freezing;
she wanted to coax someone with heat.
just like that, she shivered alone,
until the cat curled up and she scoffed at it.
just like you, she'd turn away, never free,
until the warmth left again and she cried alone.

she kept me far away;
she needed to know why we were here.
just like that, she twisted my words in her mind,
until there was nothing left of me, or us.
just like you, she'd be angry and curse, never happy,
until there was only silence and morning.

SHEWOLF

closed eyes
shaded virtue
bite first
before she hurts you

RABBIT SPAGHETTI

a spirit spread, have you
consumed patience lately?
or is it all
instant noodles and
microwave mirages of taste?
nourishment by a chase-less
prey, a thankless kill
from a thing man-made.
have you
overeaten gratification?
or are you all
slow burning, bone-in barbarossa
of chaste? satiating a godless pray,
salting tasteless fills from
poisoned wells.

TWO THINGS

one left unfinished,
the other, full,
satisfied by so little
a lover.

UNION

a friend calls and we sing
of uncertain ambitions,
honest loves, justified expectations conditions,
for captured bliss
we've performed
with different desires,
other lovers, changing ends,
but just like then,
we ascend, hopeful again

THE FIRST TIME

left to Desire
and,
clinging to fondness,
we wait.

THE SPIRIT ON THE 3RD FLOOR

a stable for my heart, built feverishly,
we're making room for me,

sobriety seems inappropriate
for the occasion,   then
an old-friend, an old-naive-friend
any-other-friend, please-friend calls
        for you

I whisper, "do you want to take this?"
        do you want to take her?

hammers and nails contain me,
I am a new-old everything,
temporary-and-barely-willing

I have had too much, and
I lecture, stampeding conjectures
after long drags of big bad dread

SARCASTIC NOTES

she's such a glamorous shadow,
attention chore—addicted to the spotlight
but she'd call it lowlight—
darkness in the torture chamber,
a continual loop, screaming
why me! fuck me! leave me!
she's irrevocably burdened,
suffering unparalleled
a gunshot in a hydrogen chamber,
"no one has ever felt like this...ever"
she goes straight through the core
to an unmatched depth, but
she's a cool loon,
don't even try to change her,
that hopeless godless prozac princess
re-gifting lessons like unwanted presents
I never want to be like her

A FINE LINE

nonsense disguised as truth
is peddled to the brightest minds,
while wisdom waits chained
in darker corners

HERE LIES

for *so* long *we* were left aware that
      our time was up,
but now it's *your* vision that
      we will interrupt.
yet somehow we're concerned about
the detriment of *your world on hold*,
I never got that courtesy when
I was thirteen years old.

no, my shine had dulled:
it's puberty, drugs, moon day, they said,
if it's not that, well, it must be in her head.
no, I was beyond bitter,
fragile like good, long-lasting things are,
shards of a stained glass window
citing a *son's* fatal scars,

and then they fined the faulty shop
that planned and made my parts
to fashion me back to *worthiness*,
a spectacle of desire; a devil *breaking* hearts.

you, that's a story worth protesting:
raping, lying, heaving, they dismiss,
it's all lies, honorable judge, she must be obsessed.
you, that's beyond bullshit, *scheming*
like low, self-serving things do,
pieces of a girl's slashed ego
slanting us to whores for hating you.

and then they fine the lonely world
that hoped and worked for art
to immortalize our coordinates,
diminish our pain and *why* we fought.

SCORPION

painted soul, you're a fragmented forgery,
wearing a bloodied crown like gilded duplicity,
the knife went in and now I'm sharpening, for
I believed we'd always be fighting together.
but you went on to disintegrating dreams
while I became the enemy, the powerful master,
the witch that slips and snipped your seams,
"in one hand a treat, the other a dagger."
are you captive or captivated by these
suicide spectacles? slow-spinning pentacles?
brazen with my witty love and unforgiving honesty?
it was too easy for you to let go of me.
but that's you, isn't it? cold and full of venom,
choking coiled so close to me, the friend that leaves.
unfriendly elixir, I think I'll always love you,
even if you hate me, haven't I always told you?
I'm better at war than idleness, lies or fear,
you, stationed far away, too indifferent to hear.
I'm at the front lines, honorable and willing to listen,
refusing to turn my spine to you ever again,
I give you my ear to make a heart, no wood or steel,
but your rejection whines, the barrel deals
through the drums and somehow still,
I'm burning when the smoke has gone.

EMOTIONAL VAMPIRE

she's got moss-lined blood
and craves chemical tastes,
watch as she crinkles that
crimson-stained pucker-face,
mocking our virtues with
excess craze, cut off her head,
another grows in its place

DEATH ROWS GARDEN

we aren't all plucked
but some of us are

with broken stems
and unseen scars

are you still blind
to who we are?

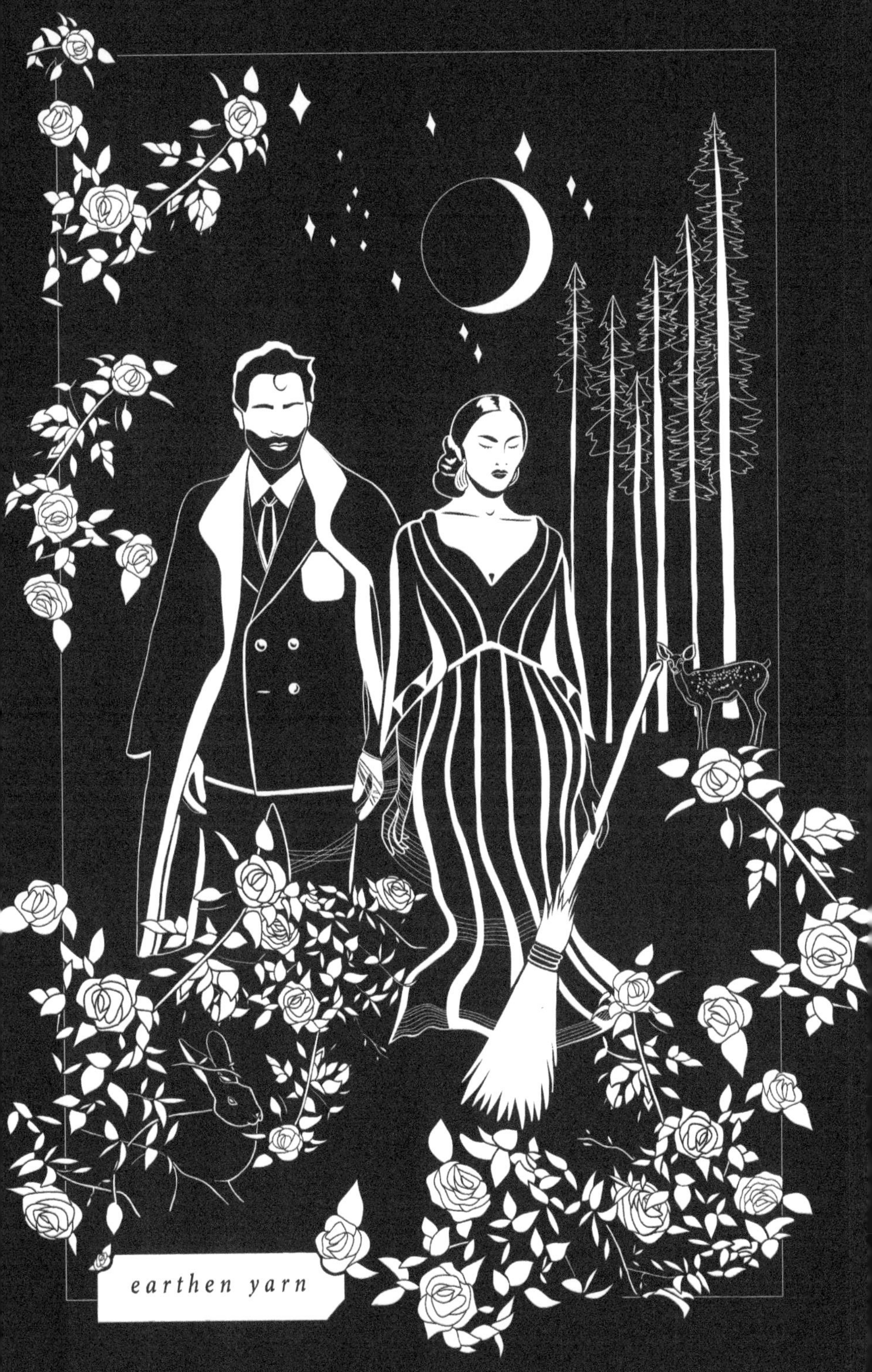

earthen yarn

SOME DAY IN APRIL

there are vintage evenings
filled to the diaphragm
with monarchs and rumors
of amorous accolades built
by spirits, risen wines
assembled by passionate moods
in giggling afternoons,
like the faultless day we spread
couture over the lawn and
filled a secret canister with riesling,
rotating molds and observations
until the toxins drowned out,
a horde of false friends' faces
bobbing in the fountain, and us,
peeling away amiable masks
to divulge unremembered foes

LIQUID PORTRAITS

we

flourish and banter
in well-nourished bliss
by loving company and tinted lips

we

stain the counter
in space and spirit
by wooden sticks and soy merits

we

wake tomorrow
in banded sunlight
by a fallen duvet
and passion replied

MONTARIA

pale night
        sewn
into a linen pocket of my
strange
        life.
I could have loved you
any
time,
        right?
but
somehow
        I love you
now
        instead of anyone
not
just
anyone
        under bashful stars
because we,
        we are fallen—us
like shaken jars
        whole and sinuous,
we
        break.

KINDRED

the dread of familial openness,
for what it is does to the
chosen,
                battered
                & fried

that bloody question
                is she good
                for you?
terrible horrible violent
                and true
she loves me, madly
much like you do

but i want your memories
                the offspring
                and tribe
we are kindred spirits
floating timelessly in our minds,
we are fleshy, full of teeth, and
                dare I say it,
                divine

BULL AND TUSK

oh, foot-pressed heart,
there's a farmhouse
in your eyes

STORYBOOK LIVING *is two-dimensional—
there's value in the sorrow—i want a flight-delayed,
burnt-chips, no-ice, wet-kisses kind-of-life. that
way, i might remember you better: your joy in a
thunderstorm; the time you dropped a bouquet of
roses on tile because you couldn't heal me; your
jumbled words and impossibly brilliant mind. if i
take a broken bone for just ten years with you, or
if i never publish another novel for a lifetime of
crumbled up paper piled in the bin, with you telling
me, "it's all divine" but i don't agree, i will have it
all. there is always a price for the magic in our lives.*

SYNCHRONY

in the inevitable syllables of blood types,
allergies, and immunities—a keen ear pressed
against my chest with wet cheeks—death's dial tone
surrenders for just a minute longer.

HAPPY TEARS II.

the first time is like butter on toast,
strange for something simple
to be so fucking good:
it's rain in a place with browning edges,
nude under a bowl of milk,
a simultaneous climax
of passion overflowed;
longer motions and careful ease
to make the impression last
and take to the body without crashing.

ØSTERBORO

have you ever been limitless?
I was once,
        in a veil of rain,
nearsighted beauty glistening by silken light
and spelled water roaming over flesh,
I became complicated by simple thoughts,
torn breathing induced by terror,
and I confessed:
        you are like god,
        but you are here, with me
        are you real?
        is any of this real?
I became lost in it,
a wrong turn on a route often travelled;
raw and unapologetically human
you looked at me, speculating conspiracy:
        how can she be so uncertain
        while knowing
        exactly what she wants?
and you told me I was safe;
there's no need to apologize;
        I see you, I really see you.
it was champagne and fresh pasta
and images of a world long ago,
lost to everyone but us—
because the divine are here
in what we remember most fondly;
when we realized it was all going to work out

it will all work out just fine

JUST THAT

topless
your mouth
        freckled
i could watch
that forever

ARTHUR

think of the way others react
to you; your hands, those
serpentine feelers, in two places
at once; evoking all emotions;
conjuring two directions; a
tangible intangibility of your
character: a dichotomy of beast
and debonair voyager, shapes
fastened in a motion of defiance;
they'll hurt eventually, they
already do.

and in this thought, react to me;
stirring fawning enraptured, I
want your oddities, I want the
way you curve a trodden path,
make it grow with wild life like
I had always been untouched,
or barren and feared, for things
are new and unbelievable when
committed by you, heating balm
between your magnificent hands
and shaping façades like clay
moldable only to the gods and
you

i am excalibur

41 DEGREES

pouring full glasses, I'll assort
these patient tea sandwiches
in neat formations, I'll invite you
to choose me over the wolves and
we can judge the world together, us
calm cucumber slices and tangy
bites of dill, our smooth butter kisses,
my mind layered by cheese anvils
and cut-off-crusts, quiet kernel smiles
we're surrounded by strange friends,
these foxes rabbits amorous animals
sunshine set for thy toothy moon to grin
at what a future we will have
and the one we are in, let's entangle
in this bed of fleece among our crumbs
and droplets of wine, in how your
autumn citrus nights are reminiscent
of my summer northern pines.

HEARTS HADN'T

unintentional friend, you dissected me,
unraveled again, thread my worry
through the eye of evil, your
spelled glances keep

I am tangled in you,
bones set by star splints.
exist here for eternity in
my uncharted soul-space,

collect maps of my freckles
while I cling to your light,
let our tongues orbit oneness,
planets forgetting collide.

DON'T DRAW MY MOON AWAY

for together we are full, we
dream of our celestial spans;
of here lies the ram and the bull.

TWENTY-FIVE

foolish to believe we have it all worked
out. harmless as it may seem, we become
fastened; turned tight to the hinges, and
when we swing, we creak and moan and
claim ourselves unmovable. it is all because
we are taught that to be stable is to be
settled; tightening bibs when we've yet
to cease spilling milk on our own chests;
pouring wine to the brim when we're drunk
enough; kissing a brand new lover because
the old one saw us for the imperfect animal
within. 'why not be renewed and spiritual
and inviting?' we think, like oil paint
on wood, forgetting the gesso. peeling
intoxicating visions of what we aren't; tears
cried for the extra inch, the ungrateful
friend, the absent minds about us. that is a
sadness i refuse to indulge. i have nothing
sorted for the first time in my life, and not
because i don't have plans or hopes and
sparks of endless wonder, but because i do.

*won't you
wash away
with me?*

THE END BITS

You made it.

Many dear friends and loved ones gave me the courage
to publish this collection. I admit that for months it felt
like a circling drain of emotion. Every morsel of myself
minced.

It started with a typewriter.

My beau searched for it. It was important to him, and
he kept the secret well. And when I went to unwrap it,
collecting and hauling the beast to my station on the floor,
I realized it had to be special. It was heavy.

Surrounded by piles of patterned paper, I received a gift
like no other. One that would keep on giving, as it had for
the owner before me. Because you could tell that someone
loved it once. Just like you or I.

This all happened in the midst of a deep love affair with
wine.

I'd always loved it, but now I was getting to know its
facets and origins beyond its allure. Case upon case, I'd
order assorted (often themed) bottles to last us the season.
With each vineyard came a story, an adventure within my
world, and I would stand at a table by a window and claw
away at the sturdy keys of my typewriter.

Many people called it antiquated, to have and use an artifact of human creation. They called it obsolete. Then why do we sculpt, pave roads, or paint upon surfaces that will be discarded? As our memories and feelings for that first love do?

It serves a greater purpose, like a spice or a matchbook; it aids the experience. And for me, the experience was an appreciation for what I could touch, feel in that moment, and it resulted in beautiful, honest prose.

There is an album, too, of instant film.

Each time I wrote, I'd commemorate my openness with a photo. Some things I must keep for myself. The practice, though, was one I'll never forget. I hadn't written anything passionate, of me, of Michelle, in so long. This was my opportunity to share something meaningful. Something raw.

I continued to add true things, sometimes traveling back in time. It made me feel more complete to know I wasn't withholding the hard things. The things that inform why the gratefulness was even there. To be alive. To be loved by someone. To have a best friend to miss. I don't regret any of that.

Countless times I reconsidered my message; the often too-passionate criticisms of the people who've hurt me, my rotating nature—wrathful then dismissive—the trauma tremors that have crippled me within physical and emotional intimacy. What could be more soul-bearing than poetry? Confessions that were never meant to leave my teapot. I added just enough fructose to conceal the bitterness, but perpetually, some of it stays.

There I'd find myself, half-dressed and cocooned in blankets, submerged in a sea of loose sheets of paper.

Not a far off image from the angst-ridden days. The ones where I'd cry and scream more than I would smile and coo. Somewhere from then to the young woman planning her life, I discovered poetry again. And I chose a different take on the same subjects. I made lists and recorded my voice, littered in long pensive pauses on the drive home. Maybe I'd have a revelation, and nine times out of ten, I didn't.

There came an empowering element to my suffering.

Any extreme could allow it to breed out of control; the doors I've broken and the evil I was too afraid to stand up to. I refuse to be wholly either end, which is why I thought this might be the expulsion of demons I needed; to feel a semblance of control in a world that ties shiny bait to romance and reveals splitting hooks to keep the fairer sex swimming in circles. I won't be filleted for anything but art.

I am not exempt in wishing for fairytale prospects.

There was a lot about Love in here. I won't deny that a balance of the horror genre and beloved animated classics turned me into a cynical dreamer. Because no matter what, I keep the mentality: 'I would survive' and 'That's me in the ballgown.'

Many have speculated that I'm the happiest I've ever been.

I think I'm the most self-aware I've ever been. That Self is more readily available, for I'm not denying Her in favor of a mask I shaped to shelter my insecurity. I'm the most unrelenting I've ever been. The bold chatter of keys sound a lot like my heartbeat when I'm anxious—I was put down by her or rejected by him or dismissed by them—the rising action of my life. A conflict that is facing retribution.

When I opened the gate, I let out all kinds of monsters.

My intentions changed. It became increasingly vital that I share the darkness to provide context to the light. It seems obvious, but it is easier said than done. I prompted myself to travel the cobblestone of my brain. That choice resulted in Arsenic & Breast Milk. This whimsical and often haunting exposé of the woman I've become, set in my twenty-five year old perspective. Thus, more than poetry was resurrected in me; a grasp on what had ached, untreated in the undercurrents of my everyday life.

There are familiar emotions that might have prompted you to read this.

My story isn't unique. I had a turbulent childhood, survived multiple assaults, was bullied and rejected by my peers, found myself in all kinds of trouble...and one day I woke up and became an academic. The suffering didn't end, but my willingness to let it define me did. I continued to experience the woes of womanhood, of the all-too-standard sexist behavior, normalizing harassment, favoritism for the males in my discipline, and shitty boyfriends. It all culminated to being essentially homeless, a gifted writer without the motivation to do anything, driving with my dog to nowhere.

Everything changed when I arrived in Orlando, Florida and set down my bags.

I admit, I was a little defeated. In a way, I had failed. I had failed at being happy. I also wasn't completely familiar with what being happy meant anyway. And hitting rock bottom sparked the Survivor again, to be resilient and pick up the pieces. I became more social, prioritized making friends and learning about my community, and I put myself out there to be shamelessly Michelle. And I fucking killed it.

I love the people in my life.

It wasn't a quick awakening, as it was suspiciously so with my ability to remain relatively stable. The source of much of my confusion for many years was the hard-earned, often unkempt, relationships and connections in my life. I struggled to connect, but never to communicate. I could describe what I felt but found it difficult to steer the velocity of my emotions. I was intense, always, and it made it hard for anyone to be close to me.

Withholding gave me a false sense of superiority.

It has become increasingly evident in the state of our culture that remaining silent on some subjects might have allowed the devils among us to thrive, without apprehension. But it was that same climate, though much quieter in terms of tangible experience being shared, that taught me the uselessness of my own hardship. There was little I could do if the adults in my life were unwilling to assist me in taking a stand: through legal action, activism, or filing a simple report.

It's about the things we don't teach and the things we do.

Everyone and no one is to blame. That's the complexity of the argument; we ask for individuals to take responsibility in a society accustomed to placing blame elsewhere. The institution blames user-error, the individual blames the institution, and so on. Where does that leave the little girl with a lot of opinions and no voice? The answer is still unclear to me.

Each time I exerted my passion relevant to these themes, I was labeled in a way that conveniently diminished my power and credibility.

To be challenged is to be offered the opportunity to alter the mind of someone seeking more information. Whether they behave like a brick wall or a permeable debater, there is always room for a lesson learned. But when it is you on the receiving end of the lecture, it can feel a lot like a condescending act of oppression, to isolate and further destroy your possibly founded argument. Where does that leave the "right" side of morality? The answer is still unclear to me.

Relativity is the only reliable explanation for why some folks seem like loons and others seem like pioneers.

It all depends on upbringing and culture, and in my opinion, genetic predisposition for ones cognitive and intellectual ability to listen and interpret an argument. The act of "shutting down" a conversation is in itself a disservice to what is Right. It is through candid debate that monsters are revealed and solutions are presented. If we are concerned with snuffing out the ignorance completely, first we must allow it to surface. Then, we must decide collectively what is to be abolished and what is to be celebrated.

The act of electing a morally corrupt individual into the institutions that decide on public morality is a problem.

This affects all of us. It's affected me. There's no way we can definitively and effectively reshape the minds of emerging generations, to thrive ethically, morally, and with loyalty to our ideals, if there is personal gain to be had in stunting those progressions.

I want to remember the state of my country and of my planet, the one that existed (and exists) while I created this collection.

It's been a depleting and terrifying time for so many: Natural and man-made disasters leveling homes and hospitals, Greedy corporations polluting our environment and denying the working class fair wages, The government

ignoring the testimony of scarred individuals for the
benefit of the Aggressors, who trade positions of power
like Pokémon cards, and the Election of a misogynistic
clown into the most powerful office in the world. These are
the things that have left me lethargic and beaten down; we
have become a country of re-traumatization and renewal of
antiquated ideals. It all drudges up the countless personal
examples I carry for each and every instance that harms
another person. And I think, why didn't I say something?
Why don't I do something? I am powerless.

This is the only power I have: my words, my vote, and my
actions.

We cannot treat an unseen illness, which is why we must
open ourselves up. Risk exposure and share under harsh
lighting the tarring organs that are failing. To understand
the intricacies of consequence; of what we ignore and
the injustices that infect us. To face the rampant and
aggressive viruses, extract their structures and deactivate
their power, act as antibodies that prioritize empathy and
forward-thinking. To restore a healthy environment of
cooperating parts.

Light your fires and explain over the crackling embers
to your children, your friends, your parents, your peers,
why women must be heard, believed, and honored for the
badasses we are.

Teach them that the whims of any individual—by greed or
a vice equally damaging—should never precede the greater
good of an innocent. Because there are brilliant and
hopeful souls who are pressed down and their gills clipped
in pursuit of a mirrored world that will surely crack
unless we shift.

Our atmosphere is thinning and our oceans are rising
quicker than our rights and reparations paid.

The silver lining lies on the interlocked hands of allies; of individuals who form a community to evoke change from the smallest burrows to the anthills of the largest cities in the world. It is the emphasis on the local economy, deterring focus from the money pit of fast-fashion, abandoning (or reducing) nonsensical means of transportation, and teaching each other in the moment that a behavior is to be abolished. We need to stop treating unnecessary suffering like a rite of passage, to cease favoring silence in service of our oppressor's comfort, and rewire the integrated and systematic mindsets that prevent us from enjoying true safety in numbers.

These are the piles through which I sifted during the making of this book.

Think of this departing fleet of concerns and observations as the concealed chair in the corner of the room mounted with laundry, clean and soiled, that remains for months. It grows and grows, hardly making much structural sense, but the existence of it both weighs and soothes in a peculiar fashion. Think of this as the dismantling of that avoided chore and the sorting of the how and the why it came to be at all.

Thank you for engaging, and a final acknowledgement of the souls who assisted me...

To my mother, Pamela, for teaching me that it is never too late to be unapologetically myself; to learn and thrive in my interests, passions; that loving someone unconditionally starts with forgiveness. To my father, Michael, for telling me I was a witch when I was a little girl; for giving me and Marina private art lessons; for supporting my decision to become a writer. To my sister, Marina, for setting an example of what it means to be a good friend; for believing that I'm strong; for challenging me to be a better person. And to Kyle, my lovely and giving partner in life, for motivating me to be a cooler human; for being curious about my mind, feelings; for keeping me busy as I try to figure you out.

And to you, the person reading this, for supporting my artwork; for influencing change, be it small or large, in the world around you; for taking it upon yourself to devote a piece of your magnificent life to indulging this modest collection.

Until we meet again,

Michelle Athena Norton

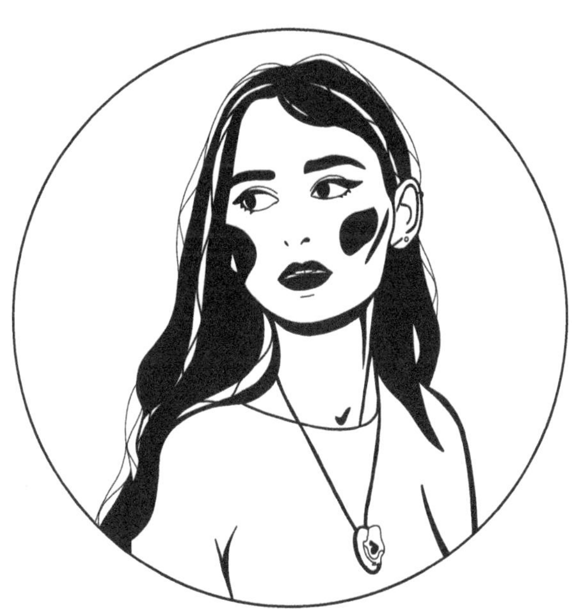